T0333804

THE
ROMNEY
MARSH
COASTLINE
FROM HYTHE TO DUNGENESS

DAVID SINGLETON

The
History
Press

First published 2008

Reprinted 2009, 2013

The History Press
The Mill, Brimscombe Port,
Stroud, Gloucestershire, GL5 2QG
www.thehistorypress.co.uk

British Library Cataloguing in Publication Data
A catalogue record for this book is available from the
British Library.

ISBN 978-07509-4849-4

Typeset in 10.5/13.5 Photina.
Typesetting and origination by
The History Press.
Printed and bound in England.

To my parents

ABOUT THE AUTHOR

David Singleton was born in 1949 at Littlestone-on-Sea in a row of cottages converted from the former Golf Club House. He was baptised at the church of St Nicholas and attended New Romney C of E School before his family moved to London. A keen golf historian, he has written the Centenary Commemoration of Holtye Golf Club near his home at East Grinstead, where he has lived with his wife for the past thirty years. His vast collection of postcards and memorabilia on which this book is based reflects a life-long love of Romney Marsh.

The Parade, Littlestone-on-Sea, *c.* 1930s.

CONTENTS

Hythe Beach, *c.* 1909.

FOREWORD

Theidea for this book came from the many books and pamphlets I have collected on the county of Kent and Romney Marsh over a long period of time. I admire, in particular, the doyenne of all the local Romney Marsh historians, the late Miss Anne Roper, closely followed by the wonderful photographic books of Mr Edward Carpenter from Lydd.

This book is not intended as a historic reference work or a guide book, but more as a walk down memory lane using as its inspiration these magnificent views from postcards and a few personal photographs from yesteryear.

I started collecting Romney Marsh coastline postcards in the early 1990s and as my collection got larger, I realised I had in my possession many wonderful images that had not previously been published in any of the earlier Romney Marsh books. I decided I would like to share these bygone images with everyone who is captivated by the Romney Marsh area whether they were born there, moved to the area or just enjoy visiting this historic coastline.

David Singleton, 2008

Dungeness Lighthouse and Signal Station, *c.* 1960.

INTRODUCTION

There are few places as alluring and mysterious as Romney Marsh, an area steeped in a history of its own and guardedly jealous of a heritage without parallel elsewhere. Reclaimed land from the sea and climatic forces have produced a coastline that is identifiable only with the Marsh; both coast and marsh are juxtaposed in partnership, the products of one another. Playing as children in our back garden at Littlestone in the early 1950s, my two smaller brothers and I would dig up shells from what had been the seabed less than a hundred years previously. This is a reminder, perhaps, of the continuous change experienced by succeeding generations. Centuries earlier, the influential port of New Romney found itself landlocked after a mighty storm diverted the course of the River Rother westwards to Rye. It was hard for me as a schoolboy to imagine that ships moored alongside the church of St Nicholas from where Thomas à Becket set out in urgency to see the Pope but had to turn back because of bad weather. It has been said that we are products of our history (often without realising it) and it is through history that a community is formed.

The development of such a community – or in the case of the Marsh, communities – grew through self-supporting enterprise and services. People knew from one another who could supply what, whether it was from an inshore fisherman's catch or a poacher's quarry. Newly married, and having come from war-ravaged Croydon in 1946, my mother arrived in Littlestone (where my father was born over his parents' newsagents shop at 2 The Avenue). During an austere period of food rationing, she was amazed at the lack of queues outside the butcher's and other shops. Most things were readily available, simply by asking.

The area is rich with tales of cargo washed ashore from vessels aground, particularly on the Goodwin Sands. Crates and assorted containers were brought by the tide and deposited along the shore of East Kent. Word soon got round and locals would be on the beach to pick up what they could, dashing home not knowing what the tins, denuded of their labels, contained. All of this was cannily reminiscent of the black economy of smuggling activities of many years ago – mischievously innocent to the chagrin of the revenue men!

Communities change and so does the life that goes with them – Romney Marsh is no different – with urban development and increasing personal mobility. Older generations like mine are left with their memories. My younger brother, David, has stirred some embers from living memory about the developing coastal communities

Alice Singleton's Newsagents and Tobacconist at 2 The Avenue, Littlestone, *c*. 1948.

of the Marsh. An avid collector over many years of postcards and memorabilia, he has produced an impressive selection of images of the area. Some of the correspondence on the backs of the postcards reveals a social commentary, such as the person visiting Littlestone during the First World War who ended up dodging the bombs from enemy aircraft!

For those of you with an association with the Marsh – whether past or present – I am sure that you will recall some precious moments as you turn the pages. After fifty years living away from my childhood home, Romney Marsh remains part of me. But I am envious of David in one respect: even though I lived there longer than he did, I have no claim on the Marsh as my place of birth! However, when I make it back on an occasional visit I find that it is still captivating, perhaps an experience akin to one who is returning from exile and savouring the long-forgotten sights that once were so familiar.

Anthony Singleton
Braithwell, South Yorkshire, 2008

Chapter One

Hythe

Our journey along the Marsh Coast commences at the eastern end of the bay, within the Strait of Dover of the English Channel where the hills of the old Saxon shoreline meet with the sea, and the ancient Cinque Port of Hythe.

The origins of the name Hythe, derives from *hithe*, the Anglo-Saxon for strand or haven. Hythe was a port of considerable importance, strategic to the defence of the realm from invaders across the English Channel in the thirteenth century. However, just like its neighbours along the Marsh Coast, the port declined in status, owing to the silting up of its harbour and the retreating sea.

By the sixteenth century Hythe's importance as a coastal bulwark had declined to such an extent that the town had become a quiet, sleepy fishing village and a haunt for the illicit trade of smuggling, which reached its peak during the eighteenth and nineteenth centuries.

The defence of England during the Napoleonic Wars (1793–1815) placed Hythe back in the front line. Once again, the Marsh Coast was vulnerable to attacks and invasion from across the English Channel. Hythe now became a military town and it was feared that Napoleon Bonaparte and his all-conquering army would invade these shores.

Prime Minister William Pitt the Younger ordered the construction of the Royal Military Canal and the Martello towers to serve as a defensive barrier against a possible invasion. Fortunately, this fear never materialised and the forts and canal never saw action. In 1853, the town saw the foundation of the School of Musketry, later renamed the Small Arms School.

Hythe has now developed into two distinct areas: the Old Town, which is dominated by the Parish Church of St Leonard, and old houses and winding lanes that cling to the steep hillsides and lead down to the flat and narrow High Street; the other area is the attractive, traditional English seaside resort of Hythe, with its elegant rows of Victorian and Edwardian buildings on the edge of the Marsh Coast.

The Edwardian seafront, Marine Parade, Hythe, c. 1907.

Looking down from the slopes of the old Saxon shoreline, we see the Marsh Coast with its wide curve and sweeping bay, stretching westwards along the English Channel within the Strait of Dover from Hythe to Dungeness, 1930s.

An aerial view of the Parish Church of St Leonard on its hillside location, dominating and overlooking the Cinque Port town of Hythe, 1930s.

St Leonard's Church overlooking Hythe, 1930s. Dating back to at least the twelfth century, the church stands nobly on the hillside, built on different levels with sturdy buttresses. Lionel Lukin, the inventor of the lifeboat, is buried in the graveyard. In the distance on the coastline the nineteenth-century Napoleonic fortresses, the Martello towers, can be seen.

A macabre scene in the ancient Ossuary in the Crypt – approximately 2,000 skulls and 8,000 thigh bones are stored here. There are several theories as to where they originated. One view is that they are the remains of Saxons killed in a battle somewhere in the Hythe and Folkestone area in AD 456, while other historians believe they may be from another battle, fought against the Danes in AD 843. It is also possible that they were dug up from the churchyard when it became full in the Middle Ages and the bones were removed to the crypt, so the churchyard could be reused. Nobody really knows the truth, it is all conjecture.

The Smugglers'
Retreat, *c.* 1900.
Tales associate this
sixteenth-century
building with the
smuggling trade and
one such story is that
a lantern was sited
at the window in the
tower upon the roof
to signal to the
smugglers out at sea
or on the beach.
The front of the
building is divided into
shops, one of which
is the fishmonger's
owned by the Griggs
family, who were associated with the town's lifeboat history. The building was finally
demolished in 1907.

This Tudor-style row of shops replaced the demolished Smugglers' Retreat in 1908. Under
the canopy is Davis & Davis, house furnishers, warehousemen and safe depository; next
door was Straughan's the newsagent's and tobacconist's. The next brick-built building
housed the London & County Bank (the bank rebuilt these premises in 1912), and next is
the Town Hall. On the opposite side of the road is the butcher's shop of Axtell & Short with
beef carcasses, hanging from hooks. The High Street is busy with Army personnel strolling
around, *c.* 1919.

A busy High Street in the latter days of the Edwardian era, *c.* 1915. The Town Hall was built in 1794 on the site of the original Court Hall. This classical-styled building with Tuscan columns was used as a court house, and had a small gaol until the latter part of the nineteenth century. The clock on the pediment was mounted in 1871.

The steps up Church Hill replaced the original slope in 1900. The old building is the Hospital of St Bartholomew's, built in the fourteenth century. It is thought that Bartholomew Street might have been the original waterfront before the harbour silted up and the sea retreated. The stone boulder is also believed to be a bollard to which boats were moored.

In 1891 the South Eastern Railway provided the area with an unusual transport system along the coastline – the Folkestone, Sandgate & Hythe Tramway. It consisted of a standard gauge, horse-drawn tram from its terminus in Red Lion Square to the bottom of Sandgate Hill, a distance of 4 miles. The carriages were either enclosed or open. These open-air carriages were popular with holidaymakers in the summer months and were known locally as the toastrack. The Victorian tramway was a major tourist attraction until the outbreak of the First World War and finally ceased operation in 1921. This photographs dates from about 1912.

As the seafronts of Seabrook and Sandgate started to develop, the South Eastern Railway opened a branch line to Hythe and Sandgate, off the main London to Folkestone line, in 1874. The section between Hythe and Sandgate closed in 1931 and inevitably final closure to Hythe came in 1951. This picture shows a train arriving at Hythe station in about 1950.

The Royal Military Canal was built between 1804 and 1809 as a strategic defence against invasion from the French Army during the Napoleonic Wars of 1793–1815. The canal was planned by Prime Minister William Pitt the Younger, and he was supported by King George III. It is the only canal in England with a 'Royal' prefix. In 1810, with the threat of invasion over, the canal in central Hythe started to be converted to ornamental walks, avenues and gardens to commemorate the golden jubilee of King George III.

The Royal Military Canal, now laid out in peacetime with pleasure boating, *c.* 1894. The bridge seen here is the Ladies Walk. Unfortunately, the structure no longer exists; it collapsed from the weight of spectators watching the Venetian Fête in 1895. The first fête took place in 1860 and is now held biennially.

Scanlon's Bridge, seen here in about 1900, is located on the western outskirts of Hythe. The canal was built with kinks or enfilades along its 28-mile route, starting at Seabrook and following the northern edge of the Marsh along the former ancient Saxon shoreline to Cliff End, near Winchelsea.

Soldiers standing outside the gates of the barracks of the School of Musketry, *c.* 1908. The
barracks were built between 1805 and 1810, and they originally housed the Royal Staff
Corps who built the Royal Military Canal.

The lecture room of the School of Musketry, 1908. It was here that British Army marksmen
and instructors were taught. It was regarded by many within military circles that to be
'Hythe trained' was a mark of excellence. The school opened in 1853 and the establishment
was renamed the Small Arms School in 1919. The school closed in 1968, when it was
transferred to Warminster in Wiltshire.

Fishermen's Beach and the Napoleonic defensive line of Martello towers on the western end of Hythe, looking along the Marsh Coast towards Dungeness, *c*. 1900.

A much busier Fishermen's Beach, *c*. 1957. Holidaymakers are watching with interest as the fishermen prepare to haul in one of their fishing smacks with ropes. In the background are the Martello towers. Many of these fascinating buildings have either been demolished or damaged by the sea. Also in this picture are the military ranges, with the targets mounted on the ridges.

West Parade with its elegant bow-fronted Victorian houses, 1930s. This comprised Ormonde Terrace and Rostrevor Terrace, built in the late nineteenth century as Hythe was developing into a seaside resort. In the distance, looking towards Sandgate and Folkestone, is the now-demolished building of the Moyle Tower on Marine Parade.

West Parade, *c*. 1955. Many of the disused Martello towers became occupied by the Coast Blockade (later known as the Coastguard) to combat the illegal activity of smuggling, which was rampant along the Marsh Coast. During the Second World War many of the towers were used as observation posts by the Royal Observer Corps and long after hostilities had ended some were converted into homes, as seen here.

The sea wall, facing the Hythe Imperial Hotel, takes a pounding from the stormy seas of the English Channel, 1930s.

The sea wall with the Martello towers facing towards Dungeness, *c*. 1914. Spectacular waves crash over the sea defences and deposit shingle on the road.

The white nineteenth-century building is the Sutherland House Hotel in Stade Street, 1930s. The town's brochure, 'Frontline Hythe', informs us: 'Stade, means landing place, and this street once led down to the harbour, built in the Middle Ages, in a vain attempt to replace the earlier silted-up, unusable harbour entrance'.

Stade Court Hotel, built in the 1930s, is situated on the corner of West Parade and Stade Street. Just past the hotel, the ice-cream van and parked cars is a low-lying Art Deco-style white building, the Four-Winds Café, originally the only café on the sea front. This view looks westwards along the Marsh Coast towards Dymchurch, 1930s.

The Imperial Hotel, the grandest of all the Victorian buildings along the sea front, *c.* 1906.
It was owned and built for the South Eastern Railway in 1880 at the eastern end of the
sea front on Princes Parade. The establishment originally opened under the name of the
Seabrook Hotel. The hotel was part of the proposed plans to develop the Seabrook estate,
with grand ideas including high-class villas and terraces with a pleasure pier; none of these
schemes ever materialised. The hotel struggled in its early years and was bought and taken
over by William Cobay, who renamed it the Imperial Hotel in 1901. It was commandeered
by the military during the Second World War and after derequisitioning the hotel was
completely replanned and redecorated. In 1946 the hotel came under the ownership of
W.J. Marston and Son, who were also the proprietors of the Stade Court Hotel.

An aerial view of
a modernised and
extended Imperial
Hotel, with the
slopes of the
former ancient
Saxon shoreline
joining up with
the sea, *c.* 1959.
The photograph
also shows the
hotel's golf links,
tennis courts and
gardens, with
the sea wall and
beach to the fore,

A composite postcard featuring photographs from the RH&DR, 1930s. Top left: the Argyll and Sutherland Highlanders, off duty from the Small Arms School, boarding the train at Hythe station; bottom left: passengers boarding at Hythe station; top right: departing Dungeness with the summertime open-sided carriages; bottom right: filling up the locomotive's water tank at Dymchurch station; centre: the majestic engine *Green Goddess*.

The buildings of the RH&DR station, restaurant and terminus at Hythe, *c.* 1930.

Hythe station with *Northern Chief* being admired from the platform and awaiting departure, 1930s.

The 'Bluecoaster Express' being reversed into Hythe station, past the anglers and others relaxing alongside the Royal Military Canal, *c.* 1950.

The Hythe station's last lifeboat was the RNLI Viscountess Wakefield. *She was in service from 1936 until 1940 and was launched seventeen times, saving nine lives. The lifeboat was sadly lost on the beaches while heroically taking part in the evacuations of Dunkirk in 1940. With this sad loss, the Hythe RNLI station closed, never to be reopened.*

Hythe RNLI lifeboat station with the crew and the station's second lifeboat, the *Meyer de Rothschild II*, on its launch carriage, *c.* 1908. The boat was in service from 1884 until 1910. She was launched twenty times and saved twenty-seven lives.

The RNLI *Meyer de Rothschild III* was a pulling- and sailing-type boat and is seen here waiting to be hauled back up the beach and housed in the lifeboat station, *c.* 1910. This boat was in service from 1910 until 1930 and was launched fourteen times, saving fourteen lives.

Chapter Two

Dymchurch

As you leave the ancient hillside Cinque Port of Hythe, exit the town at its south-westerly point and start your travels along the Marsh Coast, passing by the Military Rifle Ranges on the shingle banks and the ancient sea wall, which prevents the Marsh from being reclaimed by the sea.

You will also pass the Napoleonic Grand Redoubt and Martello towers. This stretch of the Marsh Coast was highly active during the heyday of the illicit trade of smuggling. As you enter Dymchurch, you will pass by the Ship Inn, famous for its connections with smuggling in the eighteenth and nineteenth centuries.

It was here that the author Russell Thorndike brought his fictional character Dr Syn to life while frequenting this hostelry himself. The village is also associated with another distinguished author, Edith Nesbit, who wrote *The Railway Children*. She lived at various addresses in Dymchurch and St Mary's Bay. She was well known locally, especially for her Bohemian dress sense and lively parties at her various homes in the village and surrounding area. She died in 1924 and is buried in the graveyard of St Mary-in-the-Marsh. Her grave is marked by a simple rail on two wooden posts.

Dymchurch is an ancient village and the Church of St Peter and St Paul dates back to the twelfth century. The name of Dymchurch is believed to originate from the old spelling of Demechurch, which is middle English and comes from the words *doema* or *deme*, which translated means judge or arbiter. As it was the headquarters of the Lords, Bailiff and Jurats at New Hall, an Elizabethan court room (on the site of an earlier Medieval hall, destroyed by fire in 1574) opposite the church, the name possibly arose from this connection.

The village is now mainly a centre for the holiday trade, with a number of holiday camps and caravan parks in the area and the added attraction of the RH&DR passing through the village.

The Victoria Inn and car park alongside the sea wall at the entrance to Dymchurch from the direction of St Mary's Bay, 1930s.

The village of Dymchurch viewed from the air, looking eastwards towards Hythe and showing the expanse of sands and rows of groynes stretching out to sea at low tide, 1930s. During the eighteenth and nineteenth centuries, these beaches were the haunts of smugglers, who landed their illegal cargoes of lace, tobacco, brandy etc. in exchange for the illegal export of Romney Marsh wool.

A close-up, aerial view of the approach to the village of Dymchurch from St Mary's Bay, showing the structures of the sea wall and the Napoleonic Martello towers, 1930s.

The Parish Church of St Peter and St Paul at Dymchurch, late 1940s. It dates back over 800 years to the twelfth century and was enlarged to its present size in the early part of the nineteenth century as the village population expanded.

The interior of the church showing the Norman arch, the pulpit, hymn number board and lectern at the entrance to the chancel leading to the altar.

The approach into Dymchurch and the High Street, c. 1930. The Victoria, on the right, reverted to its original name, the Ocean, in 1949. This name was discovered when workers carrying out renovation work uncovered the name under the plasterwork just after the Second World War. Older residents still refer to the pub as 'the Vic'.

The entrance into Dymchurch, now widened and with the properties opposite demolished, early 1960s, with holiday-makers casually strolling into the village, enjoying the relaxed atmosphere of this coastal resort.

The rear of the Arcade and bus station, *c.* 1926. Originally the Arcade was a walk-through shop selling all kinds of seaside wares. The front of the shop was on the sea wall and attracted the holidaymakers.

In 1940 the Arcade was completely destroyed by enemy bombing. This photograph shows the empty site in about 1950. On the left is the bus station and beyond is the building of the Wesleyan chapel, built in about 1880, opposite the City of London public house. This pub features heavily in the fictitious sagas of the Dymchurch vicar-cum-smuggler Dr Syn.

The Coastguard station from the Dymchurch sea wall, c. 1900. The watch-tower is housed on the roof of the Martello tower, and the open ground around is being utilised as allotments by the coastguards and their neighbours.

By 1950 the allotment site has been taken over for the amusement park, consisting of fairground attractions and a roller-skating rink. The Nissen hut in the foreground is a remnant of the Second World War.

New Hall and the war memorial, *c.* 1920. New Hall was rebuilt in 1580 after the original building was destroyed by fire in 1574. During the reign of Queen Elizabeth I, the hall was the seat of government of the Lords, Bailiff and Jurats, an ancient organisation dating back to 1252. They were responsible for the upkeep of the Dymchurch sea wall and the drainage of the Marsh, and to accomplish this a tax called a 'scot' was levied on the landowners. Those who lived on slightly higher ground, usually on the edges of the Marsh, were exempt from paying this scot, hence the origin of the saying 'to get off scot free'. The hall was also responsible for the full criminal jurisdiction of the area and housed a small gaol to keep suspected smugglers and other felons behind bars until their court trial. When required, a gallows used to be erected on the site of the Second World War memorial.

The authoress Edith Nesbit of *The Railway Children* fame, stumbled upon Dymchurch while holidaying in the Hythe area in 1893. She was so delighted with what she saw that she took up residence in the village. She stayed in various homes, one of which was in the small row of cottages in the High Street known as Dormers, next to Smiths Stores. Another residence was in Mill Road at the Old Cottage.

Mullions newsagent's and tobacconist's in Marine Terrace just past the site of the pre-Second World War Arcade, *c.* 1950. It was one of the residences of Russell Thorndike, the author of the novels about the popular Dymchurch vicar-cum-smuggler, Dr Syn, alias the 'Scarecrow', when carrying out his nocturnal activities.

The Ship Hotel, a haven for smugglers in Dymchurch during the eighteenth and nineteenth centuries, *c.* 1912. The author Russell Thorndike wrote about the exploits of Dr Syn and his gang in this hostelry and its surroundings. The side of the hotel advertises the local brewery of Mackesons & Co. Ltd of Hythe.

The Grand Redoubt, Dymchurch, *c.* 1930. This is a military structure, built for strategic defence against invasion during the Napoleonic Wars. The redoubt is a circular fort and was a supply and control point for the Martello towers. It was originally armed with eleven 24-pounder guns and the fort could accommodate a whole regiment if required. The Grand Redoubt was built between 1806 and 1809. The structure was fortified during the Second World War and is still under the command of the military today.

Martello towers were mini fortresses, inspired and modelled on defences in the Bay of Mortella, Corsica. In 1794 the British Navy struggled to overcome the capture of a tower of similar design. They were built along the vulnerable Marsh Coast between 1805 and 1808 and were constructed of brick and mortar, the wall being much thicker on the seaward side.

The towers consisted of three levels: the basement, where ammunition, fuel and provisions were stored, the first floor, where the entrance was by ladder which was pulled up and stored inside in case the tower came under siege (this level also provided living quarters for twenty-four soldiers) and the roof, which had a gun platform holding a 24-pounder cannon, mounted on a 360-degree traversing carriage, enabling it to fire in all directions.

Martello tower, Dymchurch, *c.* 1918. This photograph shows the tower being used as the Coastguard station. The semaphore flags on display are to celebrate the signing of the Armistice, the cessation of the hostilities of the First World War.

Looking from the Marsh towards the village before development took place along the Dymchurch road, *c.* 1923. The dyke in the photograph is the Clobsden sewer. The huts that can be seen near the Martello tower were used by the Army during the First World War. It was from this tower that two local volunteers, members of the Royal Observer Corps, spotted the first doodlebug V1 flying bomb to reach England during the Second World War on 14 June 1944.

The construction of the Dymchurch Wall dates back hundreds of years, possibly even longer.
It is believed that work was commenced to safeguard the Marsh Coast from the sea during
the Tudor period. Blackthorn bushes were in abundance on the Marsh and were thought to be
resistant to rotting in salt water. They were cut down and made into faggots to pack the base
of the wall with wooden stakes and then covered with clay, which baked hard in the sun. This
method of creating a sea wall was used until the gradual introduction of Kentish ragstone in
the early nineteenth century, and more modern materials in the twentieth century.

Hythe Road, just outside the village, looking eastwards with early wooden weekend holiday homes and Martello tower No. 22, alongside the ancient sea wall, 1930s. This Martello tower was demolished in 1956 for road widening.

The sea wall, looking westwards towards St Mary's Bay, *c.* 1925.

Dymchurch was a popular destination for holidaymakers and day trippers from inland towns and from London. This scene shows one of the fields being used as a car park as viewed from the sea wall, late 1940s.

These open beaches were ideal landing sites along the Marsh Coast and were the scene of innumerable smuggling runs along this stretch of coastline known as the Dymchurch Wall. Rudyard Kipling's song reminds us of these violent activities and times of the eighteenth and nineteenth centuries, when the trade was at its peak.

Five and twenty ponies, trotting through the dark,
brandy for the Parson, baccy for the Clerk,
laces for a lady, and letters for a Spy.
And watch the wall, my darling, while the Gentlemen go by!
Them that ask no questions, isn't told a lie
watch the wall my darling, while the Gentlemen go by!

The sands and sea wall, 1920s. In the background we can see a Martello tower and the row of houses known as Marine Terrace.

Dymchurch Wall and sands, looking eastwards in the direction of Folkestone, 1950s. The tide is out and the holidaymakers are enjoying the fine weather, relaxing in their deckchairs and participating in other beach activities.

Pipers Caravan Camp, 1930s. The hills in the distance on the edge of the Marsh are the North Downs and are referred to by historians as the old Saxon shoreline. The camp opened in the early 1930s for campers in tents only, then gradually caravans were introduced. Many of these caravans were made locally by Reg Wraight and Ray Smith at their builders' yard in Dymchurch. The buildings in the centre of this photograph are the male and female washrooms.

This photograph shows an assortment of different styles of caravans in their rows, with the caravanners enjoying their holidays on the Marsh Coast, 1930s. In these early days of caravanning, facilities were primitive: no hot water, no indoor lavatories, electricity obtained from the car battery and cooking by primus stove. However, caravanners were a hardy bunch and were prepared to put up with all these hardships, as this photograph shows.

A composite postcard of the Beach Holiday Camp, 1948.

An aerial view showing the buildings and layout of the Beach Holiday Camp, Dymchurch, 1948. The site is located near the Napoleonic fortress the Grand Redoubt and about a mile from the centre of the village.

The Beach Holiday Camp main entrance and reception hall, 1948. The vehicle is a Bedford coach and was operated by Newman & Sons of Hythe, organisers of local excursions for holidaymakers.

Sports and fun-day activities at the park provide enjoyment for the contestants and spectators alike, c. 1948. They are surrounded by the spartan wooden chalets used for accommodation.

An aerial view of the station buildings and train shed of the RH&DR station at Dymchurch, 1950, with the sprawling village of Dymchurch in the background.

The locomotive *Samson* arriving at Dymchurch station, 1950s. Visitors and holidaymakers standing on the footbridge and the platform are enjoying the sight and sound of the miniature replica locomotive.

Chapter Three

St Mary's Bay

Jesson Lane.

Low Tide.

Dymchurch Road.

St MARY'S BAY.

Sea Wall.

3218

Links Bungalows.

As you leave the historic holiday village of Dymchurch and head westwards you will pass through the small rural hamlet of St Mary's Bay, formerly known as Jesson, on the coastal side of St Mary-in-the-Marsh.

The area started to develop during the First World War, when the War Department built a camp for the Royal Flying Corps' (the forerunner of the British Royal Air Force) School of Gunnery. Before the First World War, the London Boys' Brigade came to the area for summer camp, sleeping under canvas in the nearby fields close to the military camp. After the war the camp was closed and put up for sale.

In 1920 the Boys' Brigade bought the camp, but they struggled to maintain the premises and they sold it to Captain J.C. Allnett who founded the Dymchurch Holiday Camp, utilising most of the Royal Flying Corps buildings.

At about this time, the Duke of York (later King George VI) started up the famous Duke of York Camps. This scheme brought together boys from different social backgrounds – from public and inner-city schools. The idea and the holiday camp were a major success in the late 1920s and early '30s.

The area expanded rapidly after the Second World War with the building of new houses like the Newlands Estate in 1950 and the creation of the hamlet's first pub, the Bailiff's Sergeant, in Jefferstone Lane. The building in which it was housed was converted from Jesson's Stores, which had been built in the 1930s. The opening ceremony for the pub was performed in 1951 by Major M. Teichmann Derville, the Bailiff of the Lords, Jurats and Commonalty of Romney Marsh, with his Sergeant at his side.

St Mary's Bay and the sea wall, looking westwards towards Dungeness, 1930s. The building on the right is the Sands Hotel and in the distance is the Victorian water tower at Littlestone-on-Sea, near the famous golf links.

The fishing smacks along the Marsh Coast were all launched from off the beach by using greased boards at high tide. A winch and rope was used to haul them ashore and back across the sand and shingle. The large boat in the picture is the *Grace Darling*. She is sitting on the shingle banking demasted, and was retired from fishing in 1922. The picture also shows a group of boys from the Duke of York Camp enjoying activities on the beach, *c.* 1925.

An aerial photograph showing the ex-Royal Flying Corps Camp, at this time being used as the Dymchurch Holiday Camp in about 1929. The name of the camp is painted onto the roof of the Berkshire Block. The buildings along the shoreline are the ex-Army huts of the Sands Hotel complex.

The Duke of York Camp with boys on the sports field playing cricket, *c.* 1930. The buildings were named after various English counties and the dormitories inside were named after towns within those counties.

The main dining hall was known as York Hall. The tables are set for the next meal and the facility is spartan and organised in 1920s military style.

This hut was the original guardroom and entrance to the Royal Flying Corps Camp, *c.* 1930. In this picture the hut is being used as the holiday camp's tuck shop. The boards outside read 'To the Flying Ground'; this was down Jesson Lane where private flights could be organised.

The Sea View Café, St Mary's Bay, 1930s. This was situated on the Dymchurch road and housed in an ex-Army hut.

The Sands Hotel, 1930s. Established in the early 1920s, the buildings were ex-Army huts, purchased from the War Department, and the complex was sited along the shoreline near the outflow sluice of the New Cut Channel.

The entrance to the Links Estate in Jefferstone Lane, just after the estate was completed and opened to the public for viewing, late 1930s. The pillars and flags were erected to attract customers to view the show house.

Links Estate, late 1930s. These flat-roofed bungalows were constructed as holiday homes and were in great demand. They were all sold very quickly when they were completed just before the Second World War began.

The sands and sea wall of St Mary's Bay, *c.* 1960. The wide expanse of golden sand attracts many visitors to the Marsh Coast throughout the summer months. The sea wall and groynes are designed to prevent shoreline erosion and flooding of the Romney Marsh. The wall is continually being strengthened.

St Mary's Bay looking eastwards towards Dymchurch, showing the sea wall and sluice of the New Cut, *c.* 1960. This New Cut is a large water channel that keeps the Romney Marsh drained of the excess water that occurs during the winter and flows out into the sea.

*The RH&DR's St Mary's Bay station was originally named and known as Holiday Camp
(for Jesson & St Mary-in-the-Marsh) after the nearby Duke of York's Camp.
Although the area changed its name and became known as St Mary's Bay in 1936,
the RH&DR did not rename the station until one year after the end of the
Second World War in 1946.*

The RH&DR Holiday Camp station, *c.* 1928. The tower behind the station building is a ventilating structure for an underground electric generating system originally installed for the Royal Flying Corps at their camp. It continued to be used until the 1930s, at the camp and the hamlet of Jesson, until the arrival of mains electricity in the area.

St Mary's Bay RH&DR station, late 1940s. The large brick-built structure was the new power station that generated electricity for the area.

Chapter Four

New Romney

As you leave St Mary's Bay and head westwards along the A259 in the direction of New Romney (known as the capital of the Marsh) you will see in the distance the very distinctive and majestic Norman tower of St Nicholas Church.

It is believed the name of Romney derives from the Saxon word *Rumnea*, meaning marsh. In 1066 William of Normandy with his invasion fleet landed on the beaches at Pevensey in East Sussex, and through either faulty navigation or information, his reinforcements attempted to land at Romney and they were repelled by the portsmen. After the defeat of King Harold at the Battle of Hastings, the Normans returned to Romney and ransacked the town in retribution.

In the latter half of the twelfth century Romney was granted Cinque Port status. The town's name incorporated 'New' to distinguish itself from Old Romney, the original port on the River Limen (now known as the River Rother), the harbour of which was silted up which meant that the port began to diminish in status. New Romney was a town on the seaward end of the quay and it grew in importance.

New Romney was itself destroyed as a port when the great storms of 1287 changed the course of the River Limen and silted up its harbour, making New Romney an inland town when the coastline retreated. Even so, the town continued to be an important meeting place for the Cinque Ports Federation.

The High Street and surrounding roads have a good selection of historical buildings dating back to medieval times.

As more land was reclaimed from the sea, agriculture became the mainstay of the economy, the rich alluvial soil of the reclaimed marshlands creating lush pasture for the rearing of sheep and cattle. Sheep-farming prospered well on these pastures and formed a lucrative export wool trade with France and Flanders. Wool became the first product on which export duty was levied and this helped to promote the illicit trade of smuggling on the Marsh. Just like the rest of the area, New Romney was strongly connected with smuggling. Many of the properties in the High Street have evidence of tunnels below ground, with bricked-up doors and entrances believed to interconnect with each other and in some cases leading to the church.

Agriculture remains an important activity in the area, with arable farming, market gardening, seed and bulb production and of course sheep-rearing still in abundance, but without the illicit trade of course!

St Clement's Church, Old Romney, viewed from Lydd Road with the well-known hardy sheep of the Marsh – known worldwide as the Romneys – in the foreground.

St Clement's Church, Old Romney, has Saxon origins. Like most churches on the Marsh, it was built on a mound to elevate it above the floodwater level. The original Saxon church was replaced by an early Norman-type church built in the early twelfth century, with an aisle-less nave and a square-ended chancel. The church was enlarged later in the thirteenth century. After the Second World War the church was in need of urgent restoration and the Diocesan authorities planned to close the church, but fortunately it was reprieved. Some restoration work was carried out, but funds were limited, and then the old church's fortune changed again – the Rank Film Organisation was filming on location and required the use of a church. The film they were making was based on the fictitious smuggling stories featuring Dr Syn by the author Russell Thorndike. The film company restored the parts of the church they needed for the scenes and when they completed filming, they donated a generous cheque to the parish, which enabled more restoration work to be carried out.

The Church of St Nicholas, New Romney. The church is dedicated to St Nicholas, the patron saint of sailors. The tower once had a broach spire that served as a landmark for shipping.

The nave and chancel. It is believed that William the Conqueror's half-brother Odo, the Bishop of Bayeaux, began building the church near the harbour wall in 1080, using stone from Caen and builders from Normandy. The main entrance to the church, the west door, is below ground level, believed to be created by the mass of shingle and mud flung inshore by the great storm of 1287. Inside the church the marks left by the silt and floodwater can still be seen on the columns.

Church Approach, just off the High Street, with the Assembly Rooms and the church tower of St Nicholas, early 1900s. The Assembly Rooms were built to house the Courts of Brotherhood and Guestling (representatives of the Cinque Ports and Ancient Towns) and was named the Hall of Ports.

On the corner of the Ashford road are the ruins of the Old Priory, seen here in the early 1900s. The priory and its Chapel of St John were founded in 1257 and once belonged to the Church of St Nicholas.

New Romney High Street and the New Inn Hotel, early 1900s. The inn dates back to at least 1381. The inn and its landlord are mentioned in the town's records; his name was Peter Newin – many surnames at this time were derived from their owner's occupation. This picture illustrates the mode of transport of the period – horse-drawn carts and carriages. On the road we can also clearly see an early street lamp lit by gas.

The New Inn Hotel with its Georgian frontage, masking the frame of a much earlier building, 1950s. The brewery supplying this hostelry is Style & Winch Ltd of Maidstone.

An early twentieth-century scene of the High Street, looking eastwards with the Town Hall and the New Inn Hotel on the right-hand side. The town has street lighting with gas lanterns on posts positioned on the road. Gas was supplied to New Romney in 1856.

New Romney High Street, late 1940s. On the right-hand side is the Town Hall, which dates back to the sixteenth century. Originally the building had an open arcade for trading livestock and in the early eighteenth century became the Town Hall. The building next door towards the New Inn Hotel is the town gaol, built in 1750. Below the gaol was the dungeon with iron-grated windows, looking out on to the pavement.

New Romney High Street looking westwards, *c.* 1919. On the left, just past the Town Hall, is a garage with a motorcycle and sidecar parked outside and on the right is the barber's shop, with the traditional striped pole overhanging the pavement. The next shop along, with the overhanging lantern, is the boot-repairers and just beyond there is a group of soldiers, probably from the camp at Lydd.

The Victoria Hotel in New Romney, with the words 'Commercial and Posting House' painted on the outside wall, *c.* 1900. A posting house was a public house or inn with stables, where horses for the postal services were kept. Above the doorway is inscribed 'J.J. Moody 1879'. James Moody was the proprietor and in the latter part of the nineteenth century he operated an early bus service three days a week (using horse and coach) from New Romney to the Metropole Hotel in Folkestone. His business was taken over by Carey Brothers in 1920, which in turn was sold to the East Kent Service in 1953.

It is believed that West Street was once part of a monastery at the western end of the town. John Southland, a wealthy local landowner, left a row of cottages in West Street as an abiding place or hospital for the elderly of New Romney in his will in 1610. This photograph dates from the early 1900s.

Store and garage owner Mr A.H. Smith poses proudly in his early motor car with his staff outside his premises, c. 1907. His business was located on the corner of West Street, at the western end of the town near the Cinque Port Arms public house.

The High Street looking eastwards, *c.* 1900. The building on the right-hand side (with the gas lantern above its entrance) is the Wesleyan chapel, built in 1836 and demolished in the 1920s. The site now houses the present Methodist church.

New Romney post office, *c.* 1951. It was built on the site of one of the two former iron forges that used to be in the town (the other was thought to be next to the Cinque Ports public house). The building now houses the town's library.

The Ship Hotel at the eastern end of the High Street, *c.* 1916. Above the doorway is the name of the brewery, Mackeson & Son, Hythe Ales.

The Ship Hotel under the tenancy of Whitbread, *c.* 1952. The foundations of the building are believed to be fourteenth-century in origin, with a Georgian frontage. The Ship Hotel, like other Romney hostelries, was regularly frequented by the free-traders of the smuggling fraternity. In the past, the Ship has also been the meeting place for the local Coroners' Court and has also held regular sheep auctions. The Ship Hotel is now operated by the tenancy of Shepherd Neame of Faversham. Also seen here is an East Kent Bus passenger shelter.

New Romney Church of England Junior School was founded in 1820. A schoolroom and house were built in Church Lane. It was one of the first primary schools to be built in Kent. After the first Education Act there was a wider choice of education available in the area and the school was extended and reopened in 1871. It survived two world wars and in the 1960s the construction of the Dungeness power stations increased the population of the area and the school struggled to cope with the large influx of pupils. Finally, in July 1974, it closed.

New Romney Church of England School football team, 1938/9. Back row, left to right: Mr Cranfield, Peter Webb, ? Ellis, Dick Colman, Bert Tyrell, Joey Masters, -?-. Front row: Dennis Polden, Jack Singleton, -?-, -?-, Mick Hayles.

New Romney Church of England Junior School with teacher Mr J.J. Smith and his third-year class, 1954.

New Romney Church of England Infants School inside the main school building, 1954.

The three classes of the New Romney Church of England Infants School, 1955. The teachers are, from left to right: Miss Plant, Miss Dooley and Mrs Wilson.

The New Romney branch line opened in 1884 for passengers and freight services.
The station consisted of a ticket office and waiting room, two platforms, a small goods yard
and shed and a water tank. In 1927 a short single-line extension went over the road via a level
crossing to deliver coal to the RH&DR. The station and line closed in 1967.

This photograph shows New Romney & Littlestone-on-Sea station before the construction of the miniature railway with a flock of sheep about to be boarded on to the train bound for the Ashford sheep market, *c.* 1907.

The New Romney & Littlestone-on-Sea, South Eastern & Chatham Railway station staff in the early twentieth century.

1.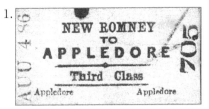

2.

3.

4.

5.

The New Romney Branch Line was owned by four different railway companies throughout its history. Above are some examples of their tickets:

No. 1   South Eastern Railway – SER, dated 4 August 1886
No. 2   South East & Chatham Railway – SE&CR
No. 3   Southern Railway – SR
No. 4   British Railway – BR
No. 5   British Railway – BR, dated 13 August 1966 on the back of the ticket.

New Romney station and a steam locomotive awaiting departure to Ashford via Lydd Town, *c.* 1958.

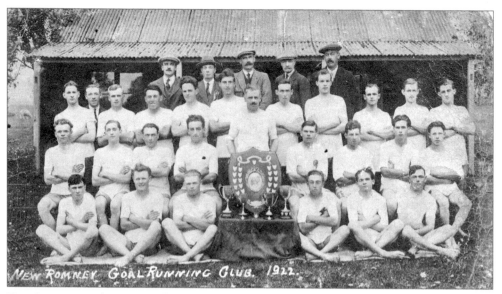

New Romney Goal-Running Club, 1922. Goal-running is an ancient sport, believed to have originated on Romney Marsh and played around the county of Kent. It was a complicated game of tag played by two teams, one side ran around a post and when successful scored a goal, while the other team, attempts to tag the leader. The main piece of equipment required was the team's flag and pole. Most team members played and ran barefoot. The sport is extinct, last played in the 1950s.

New Romney's last windmill, c. 1900. It was a smock mill that worked three sets of stones to grind corn, and was built in about 1769 and dismantled in about 1914. It is believed that there were five windmills in and around the New Romney area at one time. This windmill was situated somewhere near the old Southlands School near the present site of the supermarket on the Dymchurch road.

Chapter Five

Littlestone-on-Sea

On leaving the historic Cinque Port of New Romney, travel southwards back towards the Marsh Coast and you will arrive at the unfinished Victorian sea front of Littlestone-on-Sea.

In the late nineteenth century, this quaint promenade was a barren and desolate stretch of coastline, with only a Coastguard station and a row of wooden, black-tarred cottages nearby for the coastguards and their families to live in.

An entrepreneur named Henry Tubbs had a grandiose plan to create a new seaside resort. He was encouraged by Robert Perks, a director of the Lydd Railway Company, which had extended its line from Lydd to New Romney in 1884. Tubbs had purchased a lot of the surrounding land at the Warren and along the sea front from the New Romney Corporation. In 1886, he laid out the sea front with its hotel and a row of tall, terraced houses with wrought-iron balconies. Two years later in 1888, Henry Tubbs, with Laidlow Purves and ten other people, planned and created Littlestone Golf Course. Tubbs also had plans to build a pier at this new coastal resort, but he had problems with the planning authorities, who refused his idea, so he withdrew his plan and investment, which eventually slowed down the growth and development of this new holiday resort.

The Littlestone-on-Sea resort and golf club attracted wealthy visitors from London, mainly parliamentarians, the judiciary and stockbrokers from the City. At Charing Cross station in London posters advertised 'come to Bexhill and Littlestone-on-Sea'. Many London-based people came to Littlestone regularly to enjoy the sea, the bracing air and the golf club, and they built weekend homes between the golf links and the sea front which resulted in new roads such as St Andrews Road and Madeira Road being built. Gradually the population and hamlet grew into the small town that exists today.

Littlestone
Golf Links,
1920s.

A view of Littlestone-on-Sea from the air during the 1920s, with only the early development on the sea front as laid out by Henry Tubbs in 1886.

The Avenue at Littlestone-on-Sea was planted and lined with elm trees, creating a relaxed and welcoming arrival to the new resort, c. 1925.

The Grand Hotel and Marine Parade in about 1900. Built in the late 1880s, many of the wealthy London-based visitors stayed in these new luxurious buildings when visiting and playing at the newly founded golf club.

The Grand Hotel, Morden House and Claverly House, c. 1907. Claverly House was the residence of Robert Perks, the former director of the Lydd Railway Company, later to become Sir Robert Perks of the South East & Chatham Railway.

Marine Parade and the jubilee water fountain, 1908. The inscription reads: 'erected by Public subscription, to commemorate the Diamond Jubilee of Her Most Gracious Majesty Queen Victoria, 1897'.

The Grand Hotel, c. 1958. The building was originally the largest hotel on the Marsh Coast and was later renamed Popes and again The Ferry. The hotel survived a serious fire in the 1930s, but eventually closed and the building was demolished in 1973. In the top left-hand corner of the photograph there is a Bristol freighter aircraft on its approach to the Lydd Ferryfield.

This is an early photograph of Littlestone-on-Sea, showing Edwardian ladies and children paddling in the shallow waters at the resort, early 1900s. Not a man in sight! They are all probably enjoying a round of golf on the links.

Visitors enjoying the bracing sea breezes with the Victorian bathing huts on the shingle slopes of the beach, *c.* 1905. Bathing huts were popular in the late Victorian era when strict bathing laws were in place. They were used nationwide for modesty, but gradually public attitudes changed and by 1920 they were a thing of the past. These huts were on four wheels and the bather entered through the back, changed into their bathing costume and then the hut was pulled into the sea, for the bather to exit and enter the sea for their pleasure and exercise.

An undeveloped sea front, looking towards Dungeness, early 1900s. In the background are the bathing huts and Queen Victoria's jubilee water fountain. To the fore are the local fishing boats anchored to the shingle-ridged coastline with various fishing and shrimping nets laid out to dry on the beach in the breezy weather conditions.

The Victorian sea front with the local fishing boats on the shoreline at low-tide, *c.* 1909. A local fisherman can be seen about to go out shrimping with his 12ft net. Shrimping by local fishermen was carried out at low-tide to supplement their income. 'Romney Browns', as the shrimps were called locally, were a well-known delicacy. They were cooked, boxed up and delivered by train to Hastings and London from New Romney station.

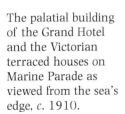

The palatial building of the Grand Hotel and the Victorian terraced houses on Marine Parade as viewed from the sea's edge, *c.* 1910.

Littlestone-on-Sea Fishermen's Beach looking towards Hythe and Folkestone, early 1900s. Just visible at the far end of Marine Parade is the water tower built in 1890 and the Littlestone lifeboat station.

The greens and beach at Littlestone-on-Sea, looking eastwards, 1930s. The tide is in and the holidaymakers are enjoying their relaxation while others are taking a leisurely stroll along the beach.

Sea barriers, the concrete-stepped sea wall and wooden groynes covered with barnacles and seaweed stretch out onto the sands and into the sea, 1950s. These were put in place to prevent the erosion of the shoreline from the enormous power of the incoming tides.

Littlestone-on-Sea lifeboat station was originally known as New Romney station. The Dungeness lifeboat, the *Providence*, was moved to the Romney station in 1861. She was in service there until 1871 when she was replaced by Romney/Littlestone's first own lifeboat, the *Dr. Hatton* (1871–84). It was followed by the *Sandal Magna* (1884–1900), *James Stevens* (1900–12) and finally *Harry Wright Russell* (1912–28). Unfortunately, in 1928 the Hythe lifeboat was in need of repair and the RNLB *Harry Wright Russell* was moved to Hythe. Later that year the Romney/Littlestone lifeboat station closed for ever. The photograph shows the commemorative plaque on the site of the former Littlestone lifeboat station.

The coastguards' watch-house and the lifeboat shed, early 1900s. In the background is the Victorian water tower, built in 1890. Also seen are the newly constructed houses of the professionals who came to visit and reside along this stretch of the Marsh Coast, and who became members of the golf club.

Coast Road, *c*. 1924. These large houses were occupied by the rich and famous who frequented the area between the wars. In the background is the lifeboat station.

Just past the coastguards' watch-tower is this house called Sandcroft, seen here in the 1920s. This was the residence of the Rt Hon Herbert J. Gladstone MP (Home Secretary, 1906–10), who was a former captain of the Littlestone Golf Club, 1896–7.

A photograph of an undeveloped Madeira Road, dating from about 1918. In the background are the water tower, Gladstone's house Sandcroft and the coastguard station flying a semaphore message.

After the development of the sea front and the opening of the golf club in the latter part of the nineteenth century, many of the visitors and members rented and purchased new homes that were being built in newly created roads in the area. This photograph depicts some of these elegant properties in the much sought-after Madeira Road close to the sea-front and golf club, c. 1930.

In 1888 Henry Tubbs, along with Laidlow Purves, the founder of Royal St George's Golf Club at Sandwich, decided to create a golf links at Littlestone-on-Sea. They laid the course out on land owned by Henry Tubbs, known as The Warren, creating an added attraction to the new resort Tubbs was developing. The club was patronised primarily by people living and working in London. The golf course was modernised by Dr Alister MacKenzie in the 1920s, who later emigrated to the USA and helped the legendary Bobby Jones to design and create the Augusta National Golf Club in Georgia.

Littlestone-on-Sea coastguards' houses in the background and the Golf Club House in the foreground, with its flagpole at the side of the 1st tee and the 18th green, St Andrew's Road, early 1900s.

Littlestone Golf Club House, *c.* 1911. This three-storeyed building with its balconies and a veranda overlooking the 1st and the 18th holes was built in 1901.

Members teeing off on the 1st hole at the Littlestone golf links, *c.* 1897. In the background on the left are the terraced wooden tarred coastguards' cottages situated on the sea wall. On the right is the watch-house of the Coastguard station.

The old 17th green sited along the sea wall near the Victorian water tower, *c.* 1920. This photograph shows what was once a barren coastline before modern development took place.

The newly formed Avenue, early 1900s. When Henry Tubbs laid out the new resort he planted elm trees down both sides of the road in The Avenue. The horse and carriage is probably carrying visitors to the Grand Hotel on the sea front, no doubt having just arrived by train at New Romney station from London.

The tree-lined Avenue looking northwards towards New Romney, late 1940s. Unfortunately, this attractive line of trees developed Dutch elm disease and had to be felled in 1981–2. They have since been replaced with flowering cherry and rowan trees.

The Avenue and the residence of Major Teichmann Derville OBE, known as the Red House, 1920s. The major was the Mayor of New Romney for twelve years, and he was also an influential member of the Lords, Bailiff and Jurats of Romney Marsh.

The tree-lined Avenue looking in a southerly direction towards the sea front, 1920s. Madeira Road is on the left and the rear view of the terraced Victorian houses built by Henry Tubbs in 1886 can be seen on the sea front.

Midway between the sea front and New Romney in the Avenue (now renamed Littlestone Road) are the local shops, built following the development of the sea front. This photograph shows the post office and Underwood's grocery store. The opposite side of the road remained undeveloped when this photograph was produced in about 1919.

The shops in the Avenue, including the Littlestone Tea Rooms and C.A. Wiles & Co., the estate agents, with an elegant early motor car parked outside, c. 1928.

The former Station Hotel (now the Captain Howey Hotel) in The Avenue, *c.* 1922. This photograph was taken before the construction of the tunnel for the RH&DR to extend its line to Dungeness in 1928.

A postcard featuring a once-common sight all over the area, a flock of Romney sheep are being taken to fresh pastures. The message on the back of this card states: 'Came here today, six miles from camp. The air-raid was close to us, I saw a good bit of it, too close to be pleasant at times, not too much damage in Hythe'. The card was dated 30 May 1917.

The RH&DR was the dream of two millionaire racing drivers of the 1920s, Captain J.E.P. Howey and his friend and competitor Count Louis Zborowski. Together they formulated a plan to build the best miniature railway in the world. The Count never saw his part of the dream come true – he was killed in an accident while practising for the Monza motor-car race in 1924.

Captain Howey and his engineer Henry Greenley continued with the plan and a site was suggested to them by Sir Herbert Walker, then the General Manager (later Chairman) of the Southern Railway, to create a miniature line along the Marsh Coast from Hythe to New Romney – a distance of 8 miles. Construction of the line began in January 1926 and it opened in the summer of 1927. The line was extended and completed to the shingle promontory of Dungeness in August 1928, making a total distance of 13½ miles.

The locomotives are miniature replicas, based on the powerful express trains of Great Britain and North America. They are one-third of full-size steam (and now includes diesel) locomotives, with top speeds of 25mph, on a 15in gauge track.

The terminus building, booking office, various sheds and the footbridge over the tracks at New Romney station, early 1950s.
The locomotive *Typhoon* and its carriages await departure.

This picture shows the Duke of York (later King George VI) arriving at New Romney station on a special train with Captain Howey and Henry Greenley, eleven months before the official opening of the RH&DR on 5 August 1926. The locomotive is *Northern Chief*, and she is carrying a trainload of VIPs. The occasion was organised to coincide with the duke's visit to his special holiday camp at St Mary's Bay.

New Romney station is the headquarters of the RH&DR. The station was originally built as a terminus until a tunnel was dug under the road to extend the line towards Dungeness in 1928. This photograph shows a train arriving on the Up line from Greatstone/Maddieson's Camp, with eager passengers on the platform waiting to board, early 1960s.

A pre-First World War horse-drawn bus. The bus operated between the Grand Hotel, Littlestone-on-Sea, and Folkestone on Tuesdays, Thursdays and Saturdays at 09.00 and returning from the Town Hall in Folkestone at 15.45. A single fare was 2s and a return was 3s. The proprietors of this service were the Carey Brothers.

Creedy House, the convalescent home in Nether Avenue, Littlestone-on-Sea, with its nursing staff and their matron standing proudly at the gates, c. 1914.

Chapter Six

Greatstone-on-Sea

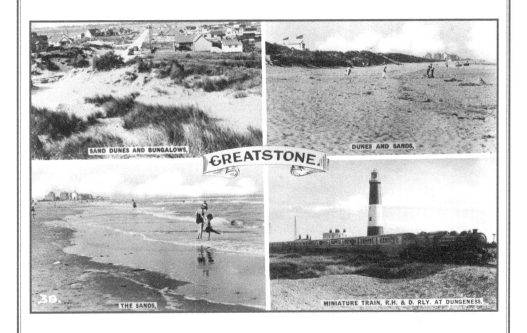

SAND DUNES AND BUNGALOWS,

GREATSTONE.

DUNES AND SANDS,

THE SANDS,

MINIATURE TRAIN, R.H. & D. RLY. AT DUNGENESS.

39.

As you leave the unfinished Victorian sea front of Littlestone-on-Sea in no time at all the narrow coastal road will take you into the vicinity of Greatstone-on-Sea. Here is a vast sandy bay and narrow strip of sand-dunes with a settlement of bungalows and a holiday camp, formerly known as Maddieson's, and now the home of a holiday park.

The origin of the name Greatstone is believed to have derived from the larger pebbles that were scoured up-channel by the tide from the direction of Hastings to form Greatstone Point. Adjacent were the smaller pebbles, which arrived from the direction of Dover to give the name to Littlestone.

Another theory is that centuries ago the entrance to the haven was marked by a great stone on the western approach and a little stone on the eastern side.

Just like its neighbours along the Marsh Coast, these vast stretches of shallow water at low tide and the sandy beaches, made Greatstone ideal for smuggling. Small boats crossed the English Channel from France and Holland to exchange their cargoes for Romney Marsh wool.

On the outskirts of Greatstone-on-Sea there are some unusual constructions, built just inland from the coastal road. These are acoustic mirrors, also known as listening ears or walls. These concrete constructions were pioneering devices to detect approaching aircraft coming across the English Channel. After the First World War more attention was given to defence against airborne attacks. Built in the 1920s, the mirrors were never used tactically and were officially abandoned in May 1939. At the outbreak of the Second World War Britain had developed a ground-controlled interception system, based on a new invention known as RADAR (Radio, Detection and Ranging), which gave vital early warnings of the enemy's approach.

During the Second World War Greatstone, along with its neighbour Dungeness, were part of vital strategic plans for the Allied invasion of Europe. The operation was known as PLUTO (Pipe Line Under the Ocean) and fuel arrived in these areas via underground pipes. Many of the bungalows and fishing shacks were commandeered by the military and some of them were gutted for the installation of centrifugal pumps. The enemy regularly sent over surveillance aircraft to photograph this part of the Marsh Coast, so great care was taken to ensure that there were no visible changes to the landscape. Pipes were wound onto enormous drums and towed across the English Channel at night and laid on the seabed after the D-Day invasions that took place on 6 June 1944.

An undeveloped view of Greatstone-on-Sea from the sand-dunes, looking westwards towards Dungeness, 1920s. The photograph shows some parked cars and the café and in the distance (just visible) are the acoustic mirrors.

A slightly more developed Greatstone, showing the completion of the new concrete road, late 1930s. The completion immediately brought in the property developers, as can be seen with the Dunes Estate Office in the foreground of this photograph.

The sand-dunes and beach with the bay sweeping westwards towards Dungeness, early 1930s.

Looking eastwards towards Littlestone, we see the front of the sand-dunes being used as a car park. The photoghraph shows the style of the early motor cars and a motorcycle and sidecar, early 1930s.

A more developed Greatstone-on-Sea looking towards the Jolly Fisherman Hotel, late 1940s. On the left is the Dune Tea Rooms, also being used as a petrol station with one of the original famous red telephone kiosks on the pavement.

The coast road through Greatstone-on-Sea looking towards Folkestone, with the bay sweeping around the Marsh Coast, 1960s.

Coast Drive, originally known as The Parade, with its new concrete roadway constructed in 1935.

With the introduction of the new road, house building increased. Houses built on the seaward side had their own private beach gardens. This postcard shows the newly built Jolly Fisherman Hotel in the right-hand corner, *c.* 1938.

The Parade at Greatstone-on-Sea attracted property developers and prospective buyers to the area. There were expectations that it would become a new town along the Marsh Coast but this never occurred because the Second World War intervened. This photograph shows the early urbanisation along this coastal road in the late 1930s.

The ribbon development of houses and bungalows along the sea front at Greatstone-on-Sea, 1930s. Many of these buildings were commandeered during the Second World War by the military and some of them were gutted and used as pumping stations for the secret military operation PLUTO.

The newly built Jolly Fisherman Hotel, late 1930s. It is believed that the name of this hotel originated from a former local ancient black-tarred building that stood nearby on the shingle beach between Greatstone-on-Sea and the Lade.

The T-junction of The Parade and Coast Drive, looking towards an undeveloped Dunes Road with the Jolly Fisherman Hotel in the centre, late 1930s.

A view showing the Jolly Fisherman Hotel, Greatstone Stores and the Dunes Estate Office, looking west towards Dungeness, 1950s.

The Jolly Fisherman Hotel, looking towards Littlestone-on-sea, c. 1965. The photograph also shows an aircraft on its approach to landing at the nearby Lydd Ferryfield.

The sand-dunes and the art-deco style architecture of the early house-building developments along the Greatstone-on-Sea coastline, late 1930s. The houses had back gardens that stretched down onto the beach, looking towards the Victorian sea front of Littlestone with the hills of the North Downs bordering the Romney Marsh in the distance.

Pre-Second World War conservation of sand-dunes appears not to have been of any concern, as the dunes here are being used as a car park, 1930s.

The dunes and expansive sands create a popular and safe bathing area. This scene is looking east towards Hythe, Sandgate and Folkestone, early 1950s.

Maddieson's Holiday Camp

The reception hall at Maddieson's Holiday Camp, *c.* 1951. The camp was created in the early 1930s and was extremely popular with Londoners. Many of the holidaymakers would arrive by train, as the Southern Railway operated a service to the camp. The station was reduced to a halt in 1954 and the main line finally closed in 1967.

This photograph shows the beach and bungalows near Maddieson's Holiday Camp, situated between the sand-dunes to the east at Greatstone and the foreland of Dungeness to the west, *c.* 1950.

The main entrance and car park near the reception hall at Maddieson's Holiday Camp, 1930s. Although the camp was situated at Greatstone, in its heyday it was known as Littlestone Holiday Camp. In the foreground the children between the parked cars are seen riding a four-wheeled seated bike – it was not unusual to see holidaymakers on these bikes throughout the Marsh area in the summer months.

A postcard of the ballroom at Maddieson's in about 1965. The camp was commandeered by the Army during the Second World War and the large ballroom was used for entertainment by the visiting ENSA (Entertainment National Services Association) groups. Just before the D-Day operation began the famous 'Lass from Rochdale', Miss Gracie Fields, entertained the troops and was given a tremendous ovation.

The bowling green surrounded by the chalets, *c.* 1960.

The simple and basic wooden chalets and the play area at Maddieson's, *c.* 1964. Holiday camps provided an all-in holiday for the family. Youngsters could go off and enjoy themselves without any worries and a variety of different sports, entertainments and competitions were on offer at no extra charge. Parents of young children could go out and enjoy the night dancing knowing they could rely on the evening chalet patrols.

Chapter Seven

Dungeness

Heading west away from Greatstone-on-Sea the narrow coast road continues, but the landscape starts to change. This is the approach to the most southerly point in Kent and the largest shingle promontory in Europe – Dungeness. The land mass of Dungeness is still enlarging, created by a combination of wind and tides scouring the shingle on the sea bed and depositing itself on the Ness. This has been a continuous process over the last 5,000 years. Several feet of shingle is deposited every year onto this promontory and the Ness continues to enlarge into the English Channel. This part of the English Channel can be extremely dangerous to shipping because its deep waters are very close to land. The Ness has seen many shipwreck disasters, hence the need for a lighthouse to warn mariners of the imminent dangers in foul weathers and fog.

Dungeness has a proud history with its lighthouses. Originally bonfires were lit on the beach to warn shipping of the nearby shoreline and these were the only means of warning and assisting the passing ships and their crews. These bonfires gave way to the first constructed lighthouse during the reign of King James I in about 1615. Each year the shingle would build up and the sea would be pushed back by this act of nature and the lighthouse would end up further inland. This being the case, there was a regular need to replace them with a newer lighthouse nearer to the sea. The second lighthouse was built in about 1635 and again for the same reason was replaced in 1792. The fourth lighthouse was built in 1901 and the existing lighthouse is the fifth construction and became operational in 1961. Again the lighthouse was moved nearer to the sea because of the shingle build-up and also because the construction of the nuclear power station blocked the beam of light from the lighthouse being seen by shipping.

Inhospitable as the Ness is, it was sparsely inhabited originally by fishermen, generations of the same families have lived and worked here. Many of these people have been brave crew members of the Dungeness lifeboat rescuing many people from the treacherous seas just off the Ness in bad weather. The dwellings of these folk are mainly on the eastern side of the point, which provides a little more protection for the fishing fleet to launch their boats from the beach on the steep-sided shingle banking. It was also the case because shoals of fish could be caught close to the shore. There is no natural or constructed harbour in the immediate vicinity.

The area is also a National Nature Reserve, designed to help protect the wildlife and the landscapes of the area. Most of the shingle is now a protected area. Over 600 different types of plant can be found here, and some of the rarest moths, bees and insect life that are found nowhere else in the British Isles have made their home here. The reserve has been described as the last natural undisturbed area in the South East of England.

Within the reserve is an RSPB site. The Ness is a well-known landfall for small migrant birds and home to a vast seabird colony. Although the area looks barren, windswept and inhospitable, it is in fact a very special and important place where nature flourishes.

An aerial view of the triangular promontory of Dungeness indicating how the shingle ridges meet up with the alluvial soils of Romney Marsh, early 1950s.

The Dungeness shingle, 1920s. Seen here are the 1884 low lighthouse, the Napoleonic Dungeness Fort and an assortment of disused railway carriages. The circular building was used as living quarters for the keepers and coastguards and lighthouse number four, which opened in 1901.

A closer aerial view showing very clearly how the shingle ridges have accumulated over many centuries to extend the promontory further into the English Channel, 1950s. This creates the need to regularly rebuild the lighthouse nearer to the sea.

The Old Revetments on the edge of the coastline of Denge Marsh, *c.* 1910. This is a barricade against explosives as used in practice and training by the Royal Garrison Artillery on the Lydd Ranges.

The Dungeness coastline looking easterly along the Strait of Dover, early 1930s. Here are the isolated cottages of the fishing community with the cart tracks seen winding their way over the shingle before the introduction of man-made roads.

The third lighthouse to be built was opened in 1792. Designed by Samuel Wyatt, and based on the design of Smeaton's Eddystone Lighthouse, it was built to a height of 116ft and powered by eighteen sperm whale-oil lamps. The tower was painted dark red with white hoops. Later the base was added as quarters for the keepers and coastguards. In 1862 Trinity House installed an electric lantern, but because of the fear of a power cut, the light reverted to using oil with a larger lamp of 850 candlepower surrounded by glass prisms. The light was visible for about 16 miles. It is seen here in about 1890.

The fourth lighthouse, seen here under construction in the early 1900s. It was built by Messrs Pattrick and Co. of London and was opened in March 1904 by the Prince of Wales, who later became King George V.

Lighthouses number four (now disused) and five with the nineteenth-century keepers' quarters of lighthouse number three and shipping passing the Ness, c. 1965. Lighthouse number four is 143ft tall and was painted black and white for better daytime visibility. The light was operated by a pressurised paraffin lamp of 164,000 candlepower through a 3-ton lens, which floated on a bed of mercury.

Lighthouse number five stands approximately half a mile away closer to the shore. This slim, tall construction is a new concept in lighthouse design, the first of its type in Britain. Built by Ronald Ward and partners, it stands 130ft in height. It is constructed of pre-stressed concrete rings. No keepers are required as the lighthouse is fully automated and is monitored by Trinity House in Harwich, Essex. The light has a range of approximately 17 miles.

The first low lighthouse was erected in 1884, and is seen here in about 1900. It was constructed of corrugated metal, mounted on a wooden plinth and the building also contained a foghorn. The beam of white light was visible for approximately 10 miles. The low light was built because of the continual growth of the Ness through the build up of shingle between the lighthouse and the beach. This sometimes confused the captains of passing ships and they ran aground when passing the Ness.

By 1932 the original low lighthouse was in need of major repairs and a decision was made to renew it. The new low lighthouse and foghorn was operational until 1959, when it was demolished to make way for the construction of the present lighthouse. This photograph dates from about 1935.

After the First World War, the Southern Railway's Ashford depot transported old railway carriages to the Ness for the company's workforce to use as holiday homes. These are seen in place in the 1920s.

Upon arrival the carriages were put in place by manual labour with the assistance of wooden rollers, strong rope and plenty of muscle power. Today it is difficult to know where they are – many of them have been grouped together or have added extensions and are now permanent homes.

Onshore Fishing

There were two methods of onshore fishing: during the summer period, mackerel were in abundance and the photograph shows a method known as Seine-netting. A net similar to a Drift-net would be anchored by rope to the beach, then four men would row-out with about 300yds of net and create a half-circle. They would then wait about 15 minutes for the approach of a shoal – once the shoal had arrived within the catchment of the net the boat would be rowed back in a circular fashion to the beach and link up with the anchored rope ready to haul the catch in. This method of onshore fishing ceased to exist after the early 1950s.

Hauling in the catch, 1930s.

Soldiers from the Lydd Army camp assisting the Dungeness fishermen to land their catch and hopefully earn a decent meal for their efforts, *c.* 1912.

The other method of onshore fishing was called kettlenets. It was a method known as 'fishermen without boats'. Drift-netting was not a successful method of fishing for mackerel during the summer, as the shoals keep very close to the shoreline. At low tide a row of poles were staked out on the foreshore and nets were hung from them, first in a straight line and then arranged to form a circular bight or pound. There was an inner and an outer bight/pound. When the tide came in the shoal of mackerel were funnelled into these circular entrapments. As the tide receded and the sea became low enough the men would wade into the bight and collect the fish. These poles and nets were erected for the duration of the summer months. Most of the mackerel were transported by horse and cart to Lydd. There the womenfolk would gut the fish and pack them into boxes to be put on the evening train from Lydd station for London, to be sold at Billingsgate Fish Market.

The heyday for this method of fishing was from 1890 up until the outbreak of the Second World War. Kettlenet fishing was finally phased out by the early 1950s.

Within the bight – drawing for mackerel, *c.* 1912.

Dungeness fishing smack in rough seas, *c.* 1912.

Shipwrecks Off the Ness

The Strait of Dover in the English Channel that encompasses the Ness is one of the busiest shipping lanes in the world. Throughout the Marsh Coast's history there have been many vessels wrecked or washed ashore off the ever-expanding promontory.

A painting by Capt Q. Craufurd RN of the unfortunate capsizing of the Dungeness lifeboat, RNLB the *RAOB 1st* while attempting to rescue the crew of the Norwegian barque *Johanne Marie* off the Ness on 17 November 1893. One member of the crew was lost.

A schooner washed ashore off Jury's Gap in bad weather – another victim off the Ness.

The steamship *Cragoswald*, *c.* 1904. The ship was driven ashore in the West Bay off the Ness after an engine failure in severe weather conditions. She was later refloated with the aid of tugs and towed to the safety of Rye Harbour.

The steamship *Ford Fisher* of Barrow, *c.* 1937. The ship was washed ashore off the Lade and beached on the shingle. She was later refloated and towed to safety.

Heroes and Heroines
The local inhabitants of the Ness have always bravely served their fellow seafarers since time immemorial.

The coastguard crew of the Dungeness lifeboat the *RAOB* (Royal Antediluvian Order of Buffaloes), *c.* 1900.

The crew of the Dungeness lifeboat the *R.A.O.B. 2nd, c.* 1908. This boat was in service from 1894 until 1912. She was launched on service twenty times and saved ninety-nine lives. One of her greatest achievements came on 19 June 1909, when she landed sixty-four people off the HMS *Sappho* to safety.

The life-saving Rocket Company of Lade, Dungeness, *c.* 1893. The company consisted of local volunteers who assisted the Coastguard to rescue mariners on board stricken vessels by firing and securing a line on board. This was then attached to the Breeches Buoy to bring the crew ashore to safety.

The Dungeness RNLI has a proud history and tradition of their womenfolk launching the lifeboat. Here they proudly pose in front of their boat, the *R.A.O.B. 2nd, c.* 1912.

The Dungeness lifeboat *R.A.O.B 1st* and crew at Lydd Fête, *c.* 1894. The boat was in service from 1886–94 and was launched on service seven times saving twenty lives in total.

The lifeboat *Mary Theresa Boileau* being hauled in at low tide. She was in service from 1912–39 and was launched on service eleven times and saved a total of seven lives.

This is the RNLB *Thomas Simcox*. She was in service from 1892–1915, was launched on service twelve times and saved fifty-eight lives in total. She is seen here standing on her blocks on the steep-sided shingle banking of the Ness, *c.* 1900.

The RNLB *Thomas Simcox* being launched off the steep-sided shingle banking of Dungeness by means of using the well-greased boards, *c.* 1904.

The RNLB *David Barclay of Tottenham*, *c.* 1932. This boat was the last of the pulling-and sailing-type lifeboat. She was in service from 1915–33, launched on service ten times and saved fifteen lives.

The RNLB *Charles Cooper Henderson* being pulled-out by the lady-launchers in about 1936. She was Dungeness's first powered lifeboat. In service from 1933–57 and launched on service seventy-eight times, she saved 112 lives. She continued in service at the Dungeness station as the reserve lifeboat from 1958–75 and was launched on service a further forty-seven times and saved another eighty-two lives.

The RNLB *Mabel E. Holland* on Dungeness beach in about 1960. She was the station's first cabin motor lifeboat and was in service from 1957–79. She was launched on service eighty times and saved sixty lives in total.

This is a Rother-class self-righting lifeboat. She is the RNLB *Alice Upjohn* seen here patrolling in a calm sea in about 1980. She was in service from 1978–92, launched on service 135 times and saved sixty-six lives.

A horse and dray delivering much-needed sustenance to the local hostelry, the Britannia public house, 1930s. To allow movement over the shingle, the cart wheels have been encased.

The Britannia pub as it was in the late 1930s.

The original Pilot Inn was created from the hull of an overturned wrecked Spanish schooner in the 1640s. This ramshackle building was demolished in the late 1950s and was replaced by a new modern building. This picture is from an advertising article cleverly using the now-famed Second World War Operation PLUTO in the late 1950s.

Dungeness School was founded in about 1876. The school badge was a shield with a black and white lighthouse on a yellow background and the school motto was 'Play the Game'. When the Second World War broke out, Dungeness was declared a military zone and most of the children were evacuated. Eventually the school closed in 1940, never to be reopened.

In the 1870s Dungeness was being considered as the site for a new harbour. Sir Edward Watkin, Chairman of the South Eastern Railway, wanted to build a new cross-channel steamer service between Dungeness and the French fishing port at Le Treport. To achieve this it would require a new rail route to be built between London and Dungeness, claiming if achieved it would be the most direct route from London to Paris.

In 1881 a railway line was constructed from Appledore to Lydd and onwards to the terminus at Dungeness, where the station opened in 1883. The plan and idea was that the area of Denge Marsh had an almost inexhaustible supply of shingle, which, if dug out, could be used for track ballast, thus creating the basin of one of the most cheaply constructed dock systems in the world. The dream was never fulfilled and the scheme was abandoned in the early years of the twentieth century.

The railway company was now left with a terminus in a remote area, carrying the lightest of traffic. In the 1930s the Southern Railway, the new owners of the service, realigned the Lydd to New Romney track along the Marsh Coast, making new stations at Lydd-on-Sea and Greatstone-on-Sea for the holiday camp developments, which were being created.

The realigned track opened on 4 June 1937, resulting the closure of the Dungeness terminus for passengers. The line remained open for goods until final closure in May 1953.

Dungeness terminus and station, 1900s. This picture shows a locomotive, the platform, waiting room and ticket office.

The lighthouse and the keepers' roundhouse standing alongside Dungeness station, with its platform and station buildings, early 1900s.

The RH&DR line reached the Pilot Inn, Dungeness, in May 1928. The final extension to the lighthouse was completed in August 1928 and this photo shows the station house, café and the disused signal-box in the late 1950s.

The wind pump in the background was installed to pump water to supply the station buildings and to replenish the locomotives. In this late 1950s photograph, to the right of the train is the scar of the closed Dungeness station standard-gauge line from Appledore, which opened in 1883 and closed in 1953.

The RH&DR terminus at Dungeness, 1960s. No. 5 'Mountain' class engine *Hercules* with its livery of Metropolitan Railway Red (built in 1927), is awaiting departure.

An aerial view of the desolate and remote promontory of Dungeness in its pre-power station days, c. 1956. The runways and aircraft of the Lydd Ferryfield airport are visible in the left-hand foreground.

Prospect Cottage, Denge Marsh, c. 2000. It was the home of the late Derek Jarman, a distinguished film producer. The area is a designated National Nature Reserve and is home to rare and precious plants such as viper's bugloss, valerian, sea kale, Nottingham catchfly, sea campion and broom. In the background are the two nuclear power stations.

The the two nuclear power stations known as Dungeness 'A' and 'B', c. 2000. Dungeness 'A' is a Magnox twin reactor station, built in the first wave of civil nuclear stations in 1960 and which started production in 1965. The station was decommissioned in December 2006. Dungeness 'B' is an AGR station (advanced gas-cooled reactor) based on the design of the second generation of nuclear power plants. The station was commissioned in December 1982 and is still producing electricity.

Chapter Eight

Lydd

As you leave the windswept promontory of the Ness, the coast road turns inland and heads northwards. Gradually, the shingle starts to merge with the alluvial soils of the marshlands to which it is joined. Four miles on we reach the most southerly town in Kent – Lydd. It is believed that the origins of the name Lydd date back to the Saxon age. At that time the area was known as Hlydda and this derives from the Latin word *littus*, which translated means shore.

In its early days Lydd was an island on the opposite shoreline of the estuary of the River Limen (the ancient name of the River Rother) to New Romney. By the early 1150s Lydd was an established Corporate Member of the Cinque Ports Confederation as a limb to New Romney. Lydd suffered the same fate as New Romney when the River Limen changed its course after the great storm of 1287 silted up the estuary.

The town is dominated by its imposing church, All Saints', known locally as the 'Cathedral of the Marsh'. The church is thought to have Saxon origins. In the churchyard is the tombstone of Lieutenant Thomas Edgar, who sailed around the world with Captain James Cook and was with him when he was killed in Kealakekua Bay, Hawaii, in 1779.

The town, like the rest of the Marsh Coast, was associated with smuggling and there are many local smugglers buried here.

In the nineteenth century the town became an important military camp with its artillery ranges. A new type of explosive was tested here – it was called Lyddite, after the town. Lydd was also famed as a brewing town in the nineteenth century.

All Saints' Church stands on the corner of Lydd's wide High Street. There is evidence of Saxon origins, though the bulk of the masonry is from the thirteenth century. It is stated that the rector, Thomas Wolsey (1503–14), who later became a cardinal during the reign of Henry VIII, had the tower raised to 132ft so that ships passing through the English Channel could sight the tower as a landmark.

The High Street, All Saints' Church and the George Hotel, *c.* 1913. The hotel dates back to 1620 and is strongly associated with the Marsh Coast's history of the smuggling trade. In 1721 there was a pistol skirmish between the Mayfield Smuggling Gang and HM Blockade Officers. A century later the inn was frequented by the notorious Aldington Gang, also known as the Blues.

Coronation Square and All Saints' Church, *c.* 1910. The square was originally known as Wheelers Green, but changed its name to commemorate the coronation of King Edward VII in 1901. This photograph shows a good side view elevation of the church. The building is 199ft long, which makes it the longest church in Kent.

Local children in their Sunday best clothes, probably on their way in to the Wesleyan chapel to attend Sunday school, early 1900s. The chapel, in New Street, was built in 1885.

The High Street, as viewed from the church, shows the George Hotel and the Guild Hall on the left, late 1950s. Just above the rooftops of the buildings on the right is the triangular roof of the brewery of Edwin Finn. He began brewing in the village in 1862 and moved to the High Street site in 1878. The brewery was sold on to Style & Winch in 1921. The brewery buildings were demolished in the 1960s.

The Royal Mail Hotel, 1920s. The hotel was built in 1746 as a coaching inn to cater for the increase in travellers through the area. The sign reads 'George Beer & Co., Star Brewery – Canterbury Ales & Beers'.

The Star Inn in Station Road, seen here in the late 1920s, is one of the oldest inns in Lydd. It is a timber-framed building, believed to date from at least the seventeenth century. The board on the building's wall shows it is a hostelry belonging to Style & Winch.

Lydd Council School was built in the latter part of the nineteenth century. The school consisted of the headmaster's house, the main school building and a further classroom which was added later. This photograph dates from the 1930s.

A railway line was opened from Appledore to Dungeness, with intermediate stops at Brookland and Lydd, on 7 December 1881. This was part of the proposals put forward by Sir Edward Watkin, the Chairman of the South Eastern Railway, to create a new harbour at Dungeness. The plan barely got off the drawing board and the idea was finally abandoned in 1902.

Lydd station and goods yard, *c.* 1900.

The station at Lydd, early 1900s. Originally named Lydd station, the name changed to Lydd Town after the new alignment to New Romney in 1937. It eventually closed to passengers on 6 March 1967.

Lydd station staff, early 1900s. The junior porter is Eustace Missenden who went on to become the General Manager of Southern Railway and was eventually knighted.

Engine crew and platform staff at Lydd station in the early 1900s.

Silver City Air Ferry was inaugurated in 1948. The airline originally operated from Lympne Airfield (near Hythe) to Le Touquet in France. Lympne could not cope with Silver City's volume of traffic so the airline decided to have its own airport and Lydd was its chosen site. Construction began in January 1954 and Silver City flew its first commercial flight on 15 July 1954. Lydd Ferryfield was the first airport in the world to transport motor vehicles. It consisted of two runways on a 345-acre site and became one of the busiest airports in Europe for carrying freight. In 1965 Silver City handled 183,000 passengers and 74,000 vehicles. The boat ferries at Folkestone and Dover eventually captured the market for transporting vehicles and caused its demise. Today the airport is used for private, light commercial and training purposes.

A Bristol freighter on the tarmac at Lydd Ferryfield being loaded with its cargo of cars, *c.* 1956. The airport's control tower can be seen in the background.

A Bristol freighter is seen here refuelling and loading its valuable cargo in preparation for take-off, *c.* 1960. In the distance are the 1930s experimental acoustic mirrors – early pioneering devices to detect aircraft approaching across the English Channel before the invention of RADAR in 1939.

A Silver City Air Ferry crossing over the French coast, *c.* 1955. This aeroplane could carry three cars and twenty passengers, as well as cycles and motorcycles.

Army Camp

Aerial view of Lydd town, taken from the tower of All Saints' Church with the site of the army camp in the distance, early 1900s.

Military camp at Lydd, *c.* 1907. During the latter part of the nineteenth century Lydd became an important military town. The camp was occupied by the Siege Artillery School. The troops were originally housed under canvas in bell-tents.

In 1906 permanent huts were constructed as accommodation for the troops. The camp became known as 'Tintown' to the troops and local people.

Troops and horses at Lydd station, *c.* 1911. Special trains to the station were used by the Army for the transportation of men and the huge numbers of horses required to haul the limber and field gun and various other heavy wagons and equipment.

The railway network reached Lydd in 1881 and the line was extended to the camp in 1883. The site was officially known as the Lydd Military Railway until 1927. It is seen here in about 1916.

The Royal Garrison Artillery preparing to unload a 4.7in gun in the sidings of the Lydd Military Camp, *c.* 1917.

A battery of 4.7in guns of the Royal Garrison Artillery practising on Lydd Ranges, *c.* 1917. They are firing at the revetments near the coastline on Denge Marsh.

The Royal Garrison Artillery excavating and making gabions for fortified trenches on the Lydd Ranges, *c.* 1915.

The fortified trench now complete and ready for gun practice with a 9.45in howitzer by a detachment of the Royal Garrison Artillery, *c.* 1915.

ACKNOWLEDGEMENTS

T his book would not have been possible without the dedication of serious postcard collectors and dealers who accumulate vast collections to sell on to other people, such as myself. I would like to acknowledge the main dealers who I purchased the bulk of my collection from:

John Rendle, Sandgate, Kent
Bernard Mundel from the Malthouse Antique Centre, Hythe, Kent
François, Eastbourne, Sussex
David and June Gentleman, Penny Black, Reigate, Surrey
A.R. Davies, Maidstone Stamp Emporium, Kent
The Rocking Horse Antiques Market, Ardingly, Sussex

. . . and not forgetting the various postcard fairs in the south east of England and the magnificent Picture Postcard Show organised by the Postcard Traders' Associaton each year in London.

I would also like to mention a few individuals who have made donations to my collection: Andrew Waterhouse, Charles Flisher, Evelyn Kane, my cousin John Singleton and my brothers Anthony and Paul Singleton.

I would also like to thank my son Adam Singleton and Hannah Emery who gave me superb technical assistance when converting my manuscript content into digital format.

Finally I would like to thank my mother and my late father for their reminiscences of the time when we lived as a family at Littlestone-on-Sea in the 1940s and 1950s, and my wife Chris for her patience for all the hours I spent at my desk in researching, writing and compiling this book.

I have included a bibliography and have endeavoured to mention as many of the books and pamphlets from which I sourced much of this information as possible. I apologise if I have inadvertently overlooked any person, organisation or book.

BIBLIOGRAPHY

Banks, F.R., *The Penguin Guides – Kent*, Penguin Books, 1955
Bluecoaster, *The World's Smallest Public Railway – A Picture Postcard Journey*, Plateway Press, 1987
Buckland, D. and Taylor, T., *The Service Record of the Dungeness Lifeboats*, Margaret F. Bird & Assocs, 2000
Burridge, David, *20th Century Defences in Britain – Kent*, Brasseys (UK) Ltd, 1997
Cameron, Janet, *Haunted Kent*, Tempus, 2005
Carpenter, Edward, *Old Romney Marsh in Camera*, Birlings Ltd, 1984
——, *Wrecks & Rescues off the Romney Marsh Coast*, Margaret F. Bird & Associates, 1985
——, *Romney Marsh in Old Photographs*, Alan Sutton Publishing, 1994
——, *Romney Marsh: A Second Selection*, Sutton Publishing, 1996
Davies, W.J.K., *Romney Hythe & Dymchurch Railway*, David & Charles, 1975
Easdown, Martin and Sage, Linda, *Hythe in Old Picture Postcards*, Back in Time, 2002
Foley, Michael, *Frontline Kent*, Sutton Publishing, 2006
Forbes, Duncan, *Hythe Haven*, Shearwater Press, 1982
——, *The Fifth Continent*, Shearwater Press, 1984
George, Michael and George, Martin, *Coast of Conflict*, SB Publications, 2004
Haisell, Victor, *Wartime St Mary's Bay*, Victor Haisell, ND
——, *St Mary's Bay – The Story of a Seaside Village & the Lost Fishing Fleets*, Hythe Bookshop, 2003
Harding, Peter A., *The New Romney Branch Line*, Peter A. Harding, 1983
——, *Branch Lines in Kent*, Peter A. Harding, 1996
Harris, Paul, *Dymchurch in Old Picture Postcards*, Back in Time, 1998
Holmes, J.V. and Mclaren, B., *About New Romney*, Invicta Publications (UK) Ltd, ND
Hutchinson, Geoff, *Martello Towers – A Brief History*, G. Hutchinson, 1994
——, *The Royal Military Canal – A Brief History*, G. Hutchinson, 1995
Mee, Arthur, *The Kings of England – Kent*, Hodder & Stoughton, 1936
Murray, Walter J.C., *Romney Marsh*, Robert Hale & Co., 1953
Oiller, Ken, *Dungeness Remembered*, New Romney, ND
——, *Tales of an Ordinary Dungeness Man*, New Romney, ND
Piper, John, *Romney Marsh*, Penguin Books, 1950
Randle, Dave, *Romney Marsh Past & Present*, Sutton Publishing, 2005
Roper, Ann, *The Gift of the Sea*, Birlings (Kent) Ltd., 1984
Sharp, Sylvia and Lindsey, Peter, *New Romney C of E Junior School*, New Romney Old School Trust, ND
Smith, Derek, *The Romney Hythe & Dymchurch Railway – A Visitors Guide*, 2001
Smith, Victor, *Frontline Kent*, Kent County Council, 2003
various writers, *About the Marsh, Volume III*, Margaret F. Bird & Associates, ND
Winnifrith, John, *The Royal Military Canal*, Geerings of Ashford Ltd, 1998
Winstanley, Michael, *Life in Kent at the Turn of the Century*, Dawson, 1978

LEAFLETS AND OTHER PUBLICATIONS
'A Walk Around Hythe'
'A Guide to Romney Marsh & its Ancient Churches', F.M. Frith, Geerings of Ashford
'Dungeness – National Nature Reserve'; 'Frontline Hythe'
'Historic Inns of Romney Marsh', the Romney Marsh Heritage Trail
'Illustrated Guide, East Kent & part of Sussex', John Langdon
'Lydd Trail'; 'New Romney Town Trail'; 'Old Lighthouses – Dungeness'
'Romney Marsh Meanders; Cycle Rides', Shepway District Council & Rural Development Commission
'The History of Lookers & their Unique Way of Life on Romney Marsh'
'The Magic of Romney Marsh', a walks pack, Shepway District Council and the Environment Agency
'The Mediaeval Churches of Romney Marsh', the Romney Marsh Heritage Trail
'The Royal Military Canal: Walks', various organisations supported by the Heritage Lottery Fund
various official New Romney District Guide Books, Plus Publishing Services
'Walks & Cycle Routes around Hythe'
'Welcome to the Ancient Parish of Lydd'